Marginalized Indigenous Identities in Native American Literature

Marginalized Indigenous Identities in Native American Literature

Rekha Rani

Edition 2023

ISBN: 978-93-87537-22-4

Published by:
CRESCENT PUBLISHING CORPORATION
4806/24, Mathur Lane,
Ansari Road, Darya Ganj,
New Delhi - 110 002
Ph.: 011 - 23244131
Mob.: + 91 - 9711991838, 9999021668
E-mail: crescentbook@gmail.com
Website: www.crescentpublishingcorp.weebly.com

Preface

The Indigenous Peoples, living across different continents of the world, have a unique way of life having distinct culture, language, and history. Despite of these variations, Indigenous Peoples share common values which are derived from their beliefs in natural world. However, with the onset of colonialism, there came a drastic change in their culture, language and history. The colonial or settler powers have objectified them as being "discovered" by subjecting colonial expansion into their territories. This strategy of objectification has led to the loss of incalculable lives and millions of acres of land and resources. Owing to the colonial expansion, the most basic rights of Indigenous Peoples were disregarded. They were subjected to series of designed policies that dispossess them of their land and resources in order to assimilate them into colonial society and culture.

The Indigenous Peoples of America have tolerated same fate like other Indigenous Peoples of the world but it is important to remember that the roots of many social, economic, and political problems can be found in colonial policies which are continuing today across the globe. The colonial policies and practices of the white society have created a void which is often filled with nonsensical stereotypes. The creation of these stereotypes have either vilified them as savage or romanticized them as spiritual or innocent children of nature. In context of these stereotypes, it becomes a crucial matter to frame the displacement which these people are suffering with. Contemplating upon the contemporary challenges and problems faced by Indigenous Peoples, it becomes important to understand their existence in the twenty-first century.

This book is about the displaced indigenous identities of America who have been reduced as marginalized 'others' by the settler powers from Europe. The complications of marginalized indigenous identities of America and of other continents have been reflected through the mode of literature. The literary works of the authors become a dazzling array of tool to express the unheard stories and voices of indigenous peoples. The authors have raised their concern over the issue of displaced indigenous identities due to distortion of their belief system for the cultural values. The voice of the authors is an attempt to relocate the displaced indigenous identities which have been perverted due to the colonial cultural impact.

Acknowledgement

I would like to express my deepest gratitude to Sumedha Bhandari for her invaluable advise. She has remained a true source of inspiration because of her selfless and devotional guidance. I bestow my heartiest gratitude to my loving and adorable mother who has supported me during the tough times with her pertinent direction. Also, I am indebted to my encouraging father who has always pushed me ahead with his ingenious remarks. Last but not the least, I owe my hat tip for my loving brother, Deepak Batta. I thank my colleagues and friends who are also a part of this venture. Last but not the least, I am also thankful to the publisher of this book.

Contents

The Historical Underpinnings

In every socio-historical context, there exists a link between a community and its artistic productions. The social and cultural identity of a person is reflected in the ideology, beliefs and practices of the creators of material manifestations like art, architecture, music and literature. Anthony King, Canadian born British professor, posits in his work Spaces of Global Cultures: Architecture, Urbanism, Identity (2004) that the cultural identity of any community has its relation to a place which can either be imagined or real. Even, Peter Herrle and Erik Wegerhoff in "The Global and the Local" have asserted that "identity is frequently related to geographical location and a specific sense of place, a place which may be characterized by a distinctive climate, and particular geographical, cultural, linguistic, architecture, social and other characteristics" (Herrle and Wegerhoff, 222).

The profound insights of the above-mentioned authors reflect that every human being, in a community, explores his identity in the national context which is beyond his personal identity. These nuances of national identity have been examined by many post-colonial theorists, research scholars and writers. Post-colonial writers have taken responsibility upon them for representing and re-evaluating the national identity through literature, and literary criticism. The re-evaluation of national identity is a result of different nations gaining independence from colonial powers. Every nation, island, state, the neighbourhood has its own unique amalgamation of history, culture, language and tradition. It is only with the understanding of the idea of cultural hybridism that the concept of identity can be understood to communicate the lasting effects of colonial process. Cultural hybridism has its association with the construction of a new identity and helps in the emergence of new self-awareness, critique, and celebration. However, the inhabitants of a colonial territory, or formerly colonized country or province do not see themselves in an independent position, even after achieving independence from the colonial powers. They feel that their identity has been changed by the cultural notions of the imperial powers.

It is observed that the displacement of human beings is one of the consequences of war. The global conflicts due to the World Wars in the twentieth century have brought displacement to the different civilizations of the world on a large scale. Due to the global conflicts, civilians find themselves living in boundaries which were ruled by unexpected invaders. The invading culture of the colonial countries leads towards a mass upheaval and displacement of civilian populations. These displacements had been geographical, cultural and psychological which produced an astonishing range of experiences for the people.

The experiences of displacement are shared by people who have always been on move, migrating, journeying and travelling for millions of years across great distances. However, this displacement became a matter of concern in the 1970's and 1980's when the process of globalization started integrating the world with interchange of ideas, products, and other aspects of culture. In the late nineteenth and twentieth century, the economies of the world and culture started connecting very quickly. With this interconnection of the economies and culture, people from various lands and territories started migrating and moving. Most of the recorded history of migrations has shown that migration took place mainly in three forms. The first one is the elite migration i.e. from the core of the empires to the periphery for the acts of conquest and conversion; the second is mass migration from periphery to the imperial cores i.e. to the cities from hinterlands and countryside in search of work; and the last one is the expansion and contraction of nomadic societies. This migration resulted in cultural fusion where nomadic and colonized people are searching for their identity. However, International Monetary Fund has identified this aspect of moving and migrating among other three aspects of globalization (trade and transactions; capital and investment movements; and the dissemination of knowledge of globalization). The cultural fusion due to migration or movement paved way to the notion of hybridity which gained its popularity during the second half of the nineteenth century.

The term hybridity originates in the nineteenth century from biology and was employed in linguistics and to racial theories. In its most basic sense, the definition of hybrid and its derivative noun word hybridity, provided by the Oxford English Dictionary, is "a thing made by combining two different elements; a mixture." The adjective form of hyridity is used to describe something of mixed character. In the contemporary period, the term is used in a wide sense and has been scattered across many academic disciplines. In the twentieth century, the term was deployed by postcolonial theorists to describe cultural forms that emerged from colonial encounters.

In recent times, the term hybridity has been adopted by many social scientists, especially by those who are interested in migration, diaspora, transnationalism, and globalization. The notion of hybridism is also shaped by the racist assumptions about the human species. There are debates about human hybrids that hinge on questions of fertility and sexuality and reflect a widespread anxiety about sexual unions between different races (in particular, between blacks and whites; one early definition of hybrid is a child of a freeman and slave). There are arguments that rely on manifestations of infertility which are difficult to sustain despite the growing population of mixed-race. A great deal of history about the usefulness of the term hybridity in various sciences - like biology, linguistics, and postcolonial studies - has shaped its adoption in the last few years by the social scientists. The intellectuals who are interested in the concepts like migration, diaspora, transnationalism, and globalization have used the term to describe the identity of persons of mixed race or cultural origin or influence (such as migrants). The cultural production of "hybrid" persons is the process of cultural mixing that shapes identity formation and cultural production. Hybridism, thus, shares its connotations with terms such as creolization, syncretism, bricolage, borderland, fusion, and cosmopolitanism. Hybrid identities shaped by cultural products, or practices are often seen as challenging, in the essentialist norms of culture, race, and nation.

Post-colonial theorists, authors and research scholars have extended the conceptual use of hybridity to scrutinize the forms of resistance to colonialism. The concept has also been explored by many theorists in association with globalization and emergence of modern nations through the works by Homi K. Bhabha, Nestor Garcia Canclini, and Edward Said. However, the usage of the term hybridism is shaped by the linguistic models in the post-colonial studies that analyze culture as a process and a site of contestation. The most significant work to analyze the political effects of hybridity in language is Mikhail Bakhtin's The Dialogic Imagination: Four Essays (1981).

Mikhail Bakhtin, a pioneering linguist, developed a linguistic version of hybridity for referring to the ways in which language, within a single utterance, can be double accented. He has related the concepts of polyphony, dialogism, and heteroglossia with hybridism. For him hybridization is "a mixture of two languages within the limits of a single utterance, between two different linguistic consciousnesses, separated from one another by an epoch, by social differentiation or by some other factor" (Bakhtin, 358). Bakhtin in his work has further distinguished between intentional and unintentional hybridity. He contends that in case of the intentional hybridity discourse is double-voiced in which one voice tries to ironize and unmask another authorial voice within same utterance and diminishes the authorial discourse which has social and political implications. He contends that in organic hybridity or unintentional hybridity "the mixture remains mute and opaque, never making use of conscious contrasts and oppositions" (Bakhtin, 360).

The usefulness of the concept of hybridity can further be analyzed through the work of Homi K. Bhabha who is one of the important figures in contemporary post-colonial studies. He has coined a number of key concepts like hybridity, mimicry, ambivalence and difference in his seminal work The Location of Culture (1994) to relate the notion of hybidization. His work is a continuation and a counterpart to Said's Orientalism (1978) with a project of problematizing cultural identity. His central idea of hybridization has been taken from Edward Said's work which illustrates the emergence of new cultural forms from multiculturalism. He uses the term hybridity for the ways in which colonial discourses attempt to exercise the power and how that power is disrupted by subverting the discourse of colonizers. He posits that hybridity attempts to deny other pieces of knowledge by tracing the shape of colonial discourse and by rendering it inherently double-voiced.

Robert J.C. Young in Colonial Desire: Hybridity in Theory, Culture or Race (1995) asserted that for Bhabha, hybridity becomes "the moment in which the discourse of colonial authority loses its univocal grip on meaning and finds itself open to the trace of the language of the other, enabling the critic to trace complex movements of disarming alterity in the colonial text" (Young, 32). Bhabha has transformed the notion of Bakthin's intentional hybridity into an active moment of challenge and resistance against a dominant cultural power. He has translated the moment as "hybrid displacing space" which further has been extended to the concept of Third Space. Bhabha argues that transgressions occur in a "third space" that includes forms of interaction and cultural difference that challenge dominant and totalizing norms. Bhabha argues for greater critical reflection to the structure of the narratives produced:

I am posing these questions from within the problematic of modernity because of a shift within the contemporary critical tradition of postcolonial writing. There is no longer an influential separatist emphasis on simply elaborating an anti-imperialist or Black Nationalist tradition 'in itself.' There is an attempt to disrupt the Western modernity through these displacing, interrogative subaltern or post-slavery narratives and the critical theoretical perspectives they engender. (Bhabha, 345)

Bhabha has challenged the assumptions about the cohesiveness of culture which is fundamental for the make-up of one's identity. He has used the ideas of French post-structuralist theorists, especially Roland Barthes, Jacques Derrida, Michel Foucault and Jean-Francois Lyotard for challenging these assumptions about the cohesiveness of culture for making an identity. The inseparability of culture for making an identity is traditionally expressed through a series of fixed historical factors (race, gender, religion, education etc). For Bhabha, the thing that problematizes is the view of history, particularly, colonial history as a teleological and dialectical movement which can be broken down into a series of familiar binary oppositions (nature/culture, Western/native etc.). For Bhabha, the main task of cultural theory is to challenge the dialect of colonial history when it has become a discipline in which the "value of any analytic activity that is considered cultural lie in a capacity to produce a cross-referential, generalizable unity that signifies a progression or evolution of the ideas-in-time, as well as critical reflection on their premises or determinant" (Bhabha, 53).

Bhabha's concept of hybridity has its association with thought of boundary as well. The epigraph that begins the book The Location of Culture (1994) effectively from Martin Heidegger's Building, Dwelling, Thinking dispels the semantic associations by offering a productive alternative "A boundary is not that at which something stops but, as the Greeks recognized, the boundary is that from which something begins its presencing" (1). The whole book presents the boundaries abound with a series of synonymous terms: interstices, borders, liminalities, in-between states, besides.

Another term, in The Location of Culture which is of due importance is the idea of ambivalence. Ambivalence renders the idea that culture is inherent in opposing perceptions and dimensions. For Bhabha, this ambivalence has a duality in its nature, that is, it presents a split in the identity of the colonized other. It allows for a split of the beings who are hybrid of their own cultural identity and the colonizer's cultural identity. Colonial signifiers of authority only acquire their meanings after the "traumatic scenario of colonial difference, cultural or racial, returns the eye of power to some prior archaic image or identity. Paradoxically, however, such an image can neither be 'original' by virtue of the act of repetition that constructs it nor can be identical by virtue of the difference that defines it" (Bhabha, 153). Colonial presence mostly remains ambivalent by opening the two dimensions of colonial discourse: one which is characterized by invention and mastery and another is of displacement and fantasy.

The key concepts which are given by Homi K. Bhabha are of utmost importance in the Third World Literature. His concepts like cultural difference, enunciation and stereotype are intermingled with each other. The cultural difference looks upon a culture as a point where two or more cultures meet and from where most of the problems arise which are discursively constructed rather than pre-given, "a process of enunciation of culture as knowledgeable" (50). For Bhabha, enunciation is the process of utterance or expression of culture that takes place in Third Space. It is through the process of enunciation that cultural difference is discovered. This process of enunciation introduces a division between the traditional stable system of reference and opposition with the articulation of new cultural meanings, as well as by providing strategies to the practice of domination and resistance. So, cultural difference is the process of identification. An important aspect of colonial and post-colonial discourse is dependence on the concept of 'fixity' for the concept of otherness. This concept of fixity implies reiteration, strictness and an unchanging order as well as disorder. The stereotype depends on the notion of fixity. It creates an identity which stems from mastery and the defence of dominant. Another important concept by Homi Bhabha is of mimicry, which is a metonym of presence. Bhabha posits that by mimicking, people of colonized society imitate and take on the culture of the colonizers. Bhabha has referred mimicry to the idea of camouflaging by Lacan in his essay The Line and the Light, Of the Gaze "as the effect of mimicry is camouflage...it is not a question of harmonizing with the background, but against a mottled background" (Bhabha, 121). "Colonial mimicry comes from the colonist's desire for a reformed, recognizable Other, as a subject of a difference that is, almost the same, but not quite" (86). Mimicry is a sign of a double articulation, a strategy which appropriates the 'other' as it visualizes power.

The concept of hybridity propounded by Homi k. Bhabha in his seminal work The Location of Culture (1994) can be used as a base to analyze the models which are based on the pseudo-scientific models of anatomy and craniometry which are used to argue that Africans, Asians, Native Americans and Pacific Islanders are racially inferior to Europeans. The fear of amalgam of the races responds to the concern that the offspring of racial interbreeding would result in the adulteration of the European race. Hybrids have been seeing as an aberration, worse than the inferior races, a weak and diseased mutation. Nevertheless, the social transformations that followed the ending of colonial mandates, rising immigration, and economic liberalization have profoundly altered the use and understanding of the term hybridity.

Hybridity has taken new meaning during a period of the decolonization movement which emerged in the non-west countries during the twentieth century. If one goes through the history of Latin America and Native America, he/she will come to know about the colonization of these regions by European powers. The colonization began during the fifteenth and sixteenth century when the wave of Renaissance came in the European countries. It ignited the spirit for exploration of the New World which lit a fire of greed in the hearts of the Europeans. Europeans started new journeys and voyages to explore the lands and to conquest them on behalf of the monarch. Their interest in exploring the vast lands had resulted into conquest of the lands. The conquests made by them generated a wave of enthusiasm in Europe and it was evolved into the process of colonization and missionization. The process was further extended by other European nations to grab the rich lands of the natives. The colonial conquest of the natives by Europeans paved way to new definitions of lands and territories. By employing the different devices like charts, maps and other measuring pieces of equipment for division of the lands and the territories, they compelled the natives to accept the notion of division for their lands.

After a long period of the contact between Europeans and Natives, the culture of the natives underwent a lot of changes. This led towards the process of amalgamation of the culture for future generations. The new breed was the result of the contact between a European and a Native. After the protracted struggles over nationhood in Latin America, in which some elites attempted to impose a white European national identity, these nation-states adopted 'mestizaje' as their official ideology in their proposal to forge national identities distinct from the provincial status in the Spanish Empire. The ideology of mestizaje was an attempt to lessen the tensions between the indigenous populations and the descendants of Spanish colonists. However, mestizaje, as formulated in the Latin American context, is a deeply racialized concept, which has concealed the residual imperial relations and celebrates the racial diversity of new nations.

In the last two decades, Latin American project of nationhood has experienced an unexpected shift towards multiculturalism. Latin America has experienced a lot of changes since the 1980's. Mestizaje has become an important concept in Latin America to build a nation for national elites and intellectuals. It has given rise to many heated debates in polar positions. On one side, it celebrates the racial democracy and on the other, some see mestizaje as a problematic ideology which has created inequality, racial hierarchies and sought for homogenization. The racial hierarchies and homogenization of the indigenous have lead towards displaced identities in this world. Nestor Garcia Canclini in Hybrid Cultures: Strategies for Entering and Leaving Modernity (1995) has asserted that "Latin American country clubs now are the product of the sedimentation, juxtaposition and intercrossing of Indian traditions (especially in the Mesoamerican and Andean areas), of colonial Catholic Hispanism and of modern political, educational, and communicative activities" (71).

The plight of Native Americans is also worth considering for the analysis of displaced native identities. The race of Native Americans was decimated by the genocidal activities of the settler powers. Dee Brown in Bury My Heart at Wounded Knee (2005) has asserted that the second half of the nineteenth century was the period when the culture and civilization of American Indian were destroyed and all the great myths of the fur traders, mountain men, gold seekers, gunmen, cavalrymen, cowboys and missionaries from the American West were popularized (Brown, xvii). Also during the period, various assimilation acts and treaties were passed to assimilate Native Americans in the mainstream American society. However, Matthew Helmer in his article "The Indian Civil Rights Act of 1968" stated that during the early 20th century, Native Americans from different tribes began collecting resources to create a collective indigenous identity, known as the Pan Indian Movement. The Pan Indian movement fought against assimilation of Native American cultures and lands under Anglo-American rule, and helped to ease the longstanding conflicts between different tribes.

The juxtaposition and intercrossing due to colonization, globalization and various policies of colonial powers have lead towards an interruption or abolition of the culture of indigenous people of South America and North America. With the expansion of globalization in the second half of the twentieth century, the traditions, values and beliefs, which form the culture of the indigenous people, come in to contact with the other cultures with which they have no common ground except the situation in which they both deal with the subject of human existence. Every society of colonial and imperial power has sent its members as explorers, merchants, and missionaries and to juxtapose the culture of the indigenous. The Storyteller of cultural Ceremony fusion, these people feel displaced within their own territories.

Considering the fusion or juxtaposition of the culture of colonial and colonized, the chapters in the book will study the displaced hybrid identities in South and North America. The process of colonization, globalization and advancement of technologies has encroached upon the freedom and the culture of these natives. With the expansion of Native American Renaissance in 1960's and 1970's as well as the flowering of 'Boom' writers in Latin America, the problems of natives have started getting attention from various critics and writers. They have started exploring the issues of their enslavement and encroachment upon their culture by the colonial powers and imperial powers. Due to the invasion and colonization of the territories, the natives are standing on the borderland. They can neither go back to their primitive lifestyle nor can adopt the new culture due to globalization which is changing the norms and values and the culture of these natives.

By keeping in mind the cultural fusion of the natives which leads towards the cultural hybridity, the succeeding chapters will focus on the works of a Peruvian author, Mario Vargas Llosa and Laguna Pueblo author, Leslie Marmon Silko. Their works, The Storyteller by Llosa and Ceremony by Leslie Marmon Silko, will analyze the issue of displaced native identities in relation to the notion of cultural hybridity. The works of the authors have exposed the issue of the displacement of native identities and their culture due to the activities of missionaries, and imperial forces. The natives are finding various modes of resistance so that they can enhance the ways of traditional life. The chapters will be discussed from the view-point of cultural hybridism which is contextualised within a global picture. The first chapter deals with the metamorphosis of culture and identities of the indigenous people of Latin America. The novel by Mario Vargas Llosa The Storyteller thematizes the westernization of indigenous peoples through missions and through anthropological studies of linguists and Christian missionaries. The second chapter deals with Leslie Marmon Silko's Ceremony which is centered on the issue of displaced identity of its protagonist who straddles between the two worlds and becomes able to resuscitate his identity by choosing his native identity. The third chapter deals with the comparative study of the novels on the cultural and many other elemental aspects.

Metamorphosis of Identities in The Storyteller

The literature of Latin America, in recent years, is enjoying a truly international currency. The international fame of the literature can be adjudged from the point that it is enjoyed not only in the western countries but also in the whole world. The literature of Latin Americans reaches its pinnacle when the writers started representing the colonial past and highlighting its pertinence in the present. It is known that history can be created through fictional representation and the writers of Latin American literature have reflected those influences of history in a concrete manner through their writings. During the wake of the Cuban Revolution in the 1960's, many Latin American authors started writing about the conditions prevalent there and started appearing on the stage of the world. The international success of the style of magical realism in the works of Latin American boom writer, Gabriel Garcia Marquez led the literature to the new heights.

It is well-known fact that Latin America, after World War II, has enjoyed economic prosperity and this prosperity heralded a period of Latin American Boom. The movement had arisen from the political and social turmoil in Latin

America during the period of the 1960's and 1970's. The authors of the period found themselves writing for a new audience in an ideologically charged climate having a focus on the Cuban Revolution. The major works published during this period were rebellious in nature from a general viewpoint of Latin American culture. The authors of the Latin American Boom period tended to experiment with the language and mixed different styles of writings in their works. Also, the authors of Latin America were greatly inspired by the works of North American and European authors. The novels of Boom period tend to blend magical and dream-like features with the attentiveness of everyday life by launching the literature to the world stage. The period of Boom occurred when Latin America was becoming commercially successful but the works of this period tended to move away from the positives of the modernization that was underway. The Mexican author, Carlos Fuentes, in an interview in 2006 with Academy of Achievement said that "we didn't come out of nothing; we came out of a very rich tradition. That tradition coincided with interest in Latin America, worldwide interest; because of the Cuban revolution...I think we also wrote good books, naturally. If not, we wouldn't be talking here. But the publicity moment was very good, and the books were good as well, so it was a very felicitous moment for our literature."

It has been observed that power has held a considerable fascination for the novelists of the twentieth century. The fascination for power has exerted a deep influence in Latin American countries and it can be seen through the lens of certain social and political upheavals in the country. The upheavals, for many writers, have become a source to give their personal visions and expressions on power. Gabriel Garcia Marquez, Carlos Fuentes, Mario Vargas Llosa and Julio Cortazar are some of the names in Latin American literature who are the specialists of Literary Boom period and who have dealt with the theme of power in the political context. Among these prominent writers of the Boom period, Mario Vargas Llosa has acclaimed his position as an author by doing experiments in the form of the novels.

Born in 1936 in Arequipa, the second largest city of Peru, Mario Vargas Llosa is the recipient of Nobel Prize in Literature. He is one of the leading writers and intellectuals of the contemporary times whose works have defined the structures and piercing images of the society. In 2010, when he was awarded Nobel Prize in Literature, the Swedish Academy declared him the winner for "his cartography of structures of power and his trenchant images of the individual's resistance, revolt and defeat." The perception of Peruvian society and his experience as a native Peruvian has a considerable amount of influence on his works. His works are the expressions of tales full with troubles of corruption, and mercilessness. Apart from these, his novels are also haunted by an endless number of victims. As a native Peruvian, Llosa is well-versed with the realities of political oppression prevalent on the land of Latin America and has tried to depict those realities of oppression by writing the narratives. Vargas Llosa himself quotes in The Real Life of Alejandro Mayta (1984) that "since it is impossible to know what's really happening, we Peruvians lie, invent, dream and take refuge in an illusion. Because of these strange circumstances, Peruvian life, a life in which so few actually do read, has become literary" (Llosa, 246).

The themes of Llosa's works are related to various issues of Peruvian and Latin American society. In his every novel, he tries to delineate an uncompromising analysis of the society. For him, literature in general and novel, in particular, are the forms to portray the expressions of discontentment. He holds an opinion that social usefulness of any novel lies in the fact that it helps in reminding people that the world is always wrong and life should always change. Thus, Llosa has addressed the fundamental problems of human life - yearning for happiness, the presence of evil in the world, boundless ambition and secret desires of ordinary people – through his literary expressions.

Mario Vargas Llosa has authored many works of fiction which are inspired by his personal experiences. He rises to prominence with his novels such as - The Time of Hero, The Green House, Conversation in Cathedral, Julia and the Scriptwriter, The Storyteller (1966), The Green House (1968), and monumental work Conversation in Cathedral (1975), Aunt Julia and the Scriptwriter (1982), The Storyteller (1989). He has a long list of works to his credit which not only includes comedies, murder mysteries, historical novels and political thrillers but also the works of literary criticism. His novel The Storyteller (1989) needs a special attention as it deals with the universal issue of displacement of the indigenous or natives from their territories or lands. The novel thematizes the Westernization of indigenous peoples through missions and through anthropological studies of linguists and Christian missionaries. The novel is inspired from the journey of Llosa which he had made into the Amazonian basin forests in 1958. He felt that the absence of law and institutions exposed the natives to the worst humiliations and acts of injustice by colonists, missionaries and adventurers, who had tried to impose their will with the usage of terror and force. By visiting these parts of the forests, he did not find the landscape exotic but found that these natives were facing the problems of violence and cruelty at the hands of imperialists. This trip into the forest of Amazon finds a literary expression in his work The Storyteller.

The Storyteller (1989) was originally written in the Spanish language in 1987 having title El Hablador and later, it was translated in 1989 by Helen Lane, a translator for numerous authors of different languages. The title of the work refers primarily to a position of a hablador within

Machiguenga culture who preserves and recites the culture's history and beliefs to the rest of the tribe. Llosa's novel The Storyteller (El Hablador) is a fascinating and disturbing exploration of indigenous nomads of Peru's Amazon Forests - Machiguengas, and about the encroachment of modern life, civilization and values into their environment and culture. Mario Vargas Llosa frames his exploration as a quest for information about the tribe – Machiguengas.

The novel begins with the narrator, on vacation in Florence (Italy) where he plans to read the works of Dante and Machiavelli as well as to look at the Renaissance paintings. But his plans go misaligned when he discovers a small shop which has a collection of exhibit photographs. The subject of the photographs is an Amazonian Forest Tribe whose history has been a fascination for the narrator. He knows a lot about these tribes – including their myths, customs, religious beliefs and traditions. As he watches over the photographs, he is drawn to an indistinct figure of a man seating among the tribal members, gesturing and talking in a manner that suggests that he is speaking to an attentive audience - a storyteller. The most disturbing thing to the narrator happens is the fact that there is no such thing as a traditional storyteller among these Amazonian tribes in the twentieth century. He has a distinct feeling that he recognizes the face of a speaker who is the narrator's old college friend named Saul Zuratas. The tribe has long fascinated the narrator's friend Saul and once played a central role in a debate he had with him at the university, Saul Zuratas. This incident restores him the past memory of his friendship with Saul Zuratas (Mascarita) who suddenly disappeared from Lima. When the narrator looks over the photographs of the indigenous people in the Amazon region of Peru, he starts thinking about his friend Saul and the daily life of indigenous Machiguengas who have lived in an isolated world of their own, away from the civilization. But due to the impact of imperialism,

Christian missionaries, the works of the linguists and ethnographers, the daily life of the Machiguengas has changed. The instance for this has been provided by him in the novel The Storyteller as "the daily life of a tribe which, until a few years ago, had lived virtually isolated from civilization, scattered about in units of one or two families. Only in our day had they begun to group together in those places documented by the exhibition, but many of them still remained in the forest..." (Llosa, 4).

As the narrator reflects about his numerous conversations with Saul during their college days in cafes and seminars, he recalls his friend's bizarre appearance. Saul was an intense young Jewish man having a purplish birthmark that has covered half of his face and earned him the nickname La Mascarita, or Mask-face. Although he was timid and self-effacing, he was deeply concerned about the survival of indigenous peoples in Peru and had strong criticism for those who seek to evangelize, assimilate, or "culturally advance" such people under the guise of scientific, anthropological, and linguistic research. The narrator and Saul shared discussions on many issues, including the Machiguenga people. At college, Saul was an object of ridicule because of his resentment against the missionaries who promoted a kind of progress that destroyed the Machiguengas and also because of his bizarre physical appearance. After completing his graduation, he announced that he was abandoning both the Amazon and a prestigious fellowship of a research project that would give him the opportunity to study in Paris. Instead, he told his friends that he had decided to accompany his father to Israel. However, he lied to his friends because he had developed a secret plan to join the Machiguengas into the remote Amazon forests of Peru. Saul Zuratas left his past identity and went to the Amazon forests to live with these natives. The insights and motive of Saul Zuratas to reside with the Machiguenga tribe seems to be an act of love and empathy as compared to the work of ethnographers and linguists who have explored the indigenous tribes for professional or rational reasons. Nevertheless, his intentions become questionable when he could not leave behind the western dominant discourses that had influenced him "naturally, hundreds of years of beliefs and customs don't disappear overnight. It'll take time..." (Llosa, 172).

This novel deals with the major issue that is not only prevalent in Peru but also in the other countries of Latin America. The co-existence and co-dependence of the modern society which is prepared to participate in the cultural, economic and political life of the global world and of the indigenous tribes. The Machiguengas in The Storyteller are indigenous tribes who live along the banks of the Urubamba River in Amazon Forests of Peru. All over the centuries, different Christian missionaries, the linguists and ethnographers came to these territories for their conversion from the primitive mode of living to the civilized ways. But more or less for their own purpose, they are held responsible for the destruction of the culture and tradition of the Machiguengas. The strategies deployed by the Christian missionaries, linguists and ethnographers have paved towards distorted native identities.

An article in Global Forest Atlas "History of Settlement in the Amazon Basin" that the region of Amazon basin met an abrupt shock at beginning of the sixteenth century when settlers began to explore the region. Many explorers started searching the Peruvian and northern Bolivian Amazon for El Dorado (the lost city of Incas) but with the passage of time, the region became a chess-board to exploit the natural resources by the traders of imperial powers. However, the role of the ethnographers, anthropologists, and linguists for the acculturation and occidentalization of the Amazonian tribes is no less than the works of these traders. These anthropologists at the name of civilizing are imposing their culture upon them. The strategy employed by them has paved way towards the cultural hybridization. The natives residing in the Amazon forest are not able to accept the new culture imposed by the missionaries as well as they do not want to leave their native traditions and beliefs.

Vibeke Andersson in "Indigenous People – Territory and Identity" has asserted that the core subject of anthropology is the cultural 'other'. It tries to study the secluded cultures to depict them as 'others'. Hence, to study the complexities of the natives living in these societies, the complexities should be explored in the context of counter-globalization movements, and worldwide cultural confrontation. In contemporary times, it has been observed that the culture of societies is an amalgam of cross-cultural influences which are layered upon one another. The powers of imperialism and globalization have both expanded the reach of Western culture, a process in which West constantly interacts with East to appropriate culture for its own means. Thus, cultural hybridism is woven in every corner of the world from trendy fusion cuisine to Caribbean rhythms in pop music to the hyphenated identities that signify ethnic Americans, with a dominant culture blending of the cultural codes of Third World culture.

In the nineteenth century, fears of racial miscegenation have dominated thinking and governance across the globe. Miscegenation and fears for a loss of national and racial integrity have long shaped national cultures, histories, and policies across the globe. For Homi K. Bhabha, hybridity is the process in which the governing authorities of the colonials are committed to change the identities of the colonized (other) in a singular universal framework. Bhabha posits that a hybridity is a form of liminality or in-between space, where the "cutting edge of translation and negotiation" occurs and which he terms the third space. This hybridization in the contemporary period must be looked upon in the context of globalization which is influencing the cultures of the societies from the imperialistic powers making the oppressed sections feeling displaced within their culture.

The novel The Storyteller (1989) by Mario Vargas Llosa has been evolved around the theme of displaced cultural identity by focusing on the relationship among the global, national and tribal societies. This is what Homi K. Bhabha has termed as "ambivalence." The Storyteller (1989) suggests the impossibility of maintaining one's native authenticity and independence in this globalized and imperialistic world. The character of Fidel Pereira, in the novel, can be analyzed from this context. His identity is a mixture of a feudal lord and an aboriginal cacique because he is a son of a white man from Cusco and a Machiguenga woman. Fidel's father, in the last century of the nineteenth century, went into the deep forests of Amazon, where Machiguengas sheltered him and he was married to a woman of the tribe. Fidel's identity, as a son of a white man and Machiguenga woman, straddles on the two cultures. As a white man, Fidel now put this whole tribe to work and pays them nothing. He exploits them as whites have exploited the tribal members. But as he is also the member of these tribes, he protects these tribes from the others who try to suppress them. The instance of it can be referred to as "he uses them, of course. But at least he doesn't despise them. He knows all about their culture and is proud of it. And when other people try to trample on them, he protects them" (Llosa, 19).

The character of Fidel reveals that he is acting as a bridge between the two cultures, drawing them and slowly merging them from their primitive ways of life to modern ways of civilization. He can be analyzed as a creole of white and Machiguenga culture where he is able to culturally transmit the situations of displacement. Raquel

Romberg in "Revisiting Creolization" has asserted that creolization is more than mixing because it involves the creation of new cultures. Further, it suggests the symbolic take-over of symbols of the power of powerful others in situations of physical invasion and conquest.

The protagonist of the novel, Saul Zuratas, also signifies as creol character. He experiences a conversion not only in the cultural sense but also in the religious one. He belongs to Jewish religion and has a birthmark on his face which gives him a look of a monster. Despite his looks, he always remains altruistic in his behaviour. Also, his identity can be considered as a hybrid because his father is a Jew and his mother is a creole from Talara. After coming to Lima as a refugee, Saul's father married his mother. However, her mother, being a Christian, was not accepted by the members of society "the Jewish community of Lima never accepted her, even though to please Don Solomon she had gone through the ritual of lustral bath and received instructions from the rabbi in order to fulfil all the rites necessary for conversion" (Llosa, 11). The reason for her non-acceptance can be signified from a viewpoint that she belongs to a different culture and religion. Her identity can be analyzed within the religious and spatial dimension of the liminality. She is in-betwixt the cultures finding her position in the society.

The displacement of identities in the novel can be scrutinized from the problem of extermination of Jews which has caused physically and mentally distorted identities. The problem is depicted through Mascarita's father who is a refugee in Lima. The Jews after World War II had migrated to the different countries of the world in search of the place to live. Being marginal, they suffered during their search for place and identity in the world. Saul himself feels alienated in the society in which he lives. The people of society consider him a monstrous being. His association with Jewish tradition was another reason for his psychological displaced identity. Saul's perception about himself can be examined by his comment that "I'm identifying the Amazonian Indians with the Jewish people, always a minority and always persecuted for their religion and their mores that are different from those of the rest of society..." (Llosa, 28).

Saul Zuratas's psychological and physical displacement in society brings him closer to the Machiguengas who have faced the same problem. He compares himself with Amazonian tribes who bear the same fate of displacement. Although Saul is being harassed by every section of the society, yet he delineates his outer look as a happy man. Nevertheless, Saul's inner self did not make him a cheerful personality because of his alienation as a man in the society even by his father. His father has refused him to set his foot behind the counter of the shop. He uses to say that Saul will never be a shopkeeper like him. Saul asks him "But why, papa? Are you afraid this face of mine will scare the customers away?" (Llosa, 12). For these reasons, from being ridiculed by the people of society and his father, either intentionally or not, he becomes obsessed with the group of the Amazonian tribe and decides to live with the natives. He tries to acquire a new identity by becoming one with these Machiguengas. The narrator thinks in himself that "had he unconsciously identified with those marginal beings because of the birthmark that made him, too, a marginal being, everytime he went out on the streets?" (Llosa, 28).

The problem of displaced identities has been shown in the novel through the Amazonian Machiguengas also who are nature-oriented people. It has been observed that is after the second half of the twentieth century, the indigenous groups of Latin America have increasingly migrated to urban regions beyond the national borders. It is because of the political and military conflicts, encroachment on their lands, natural disasters, crises in agriculture and extreme cases of poverty and the impact of globalization on these people that lead towards the labour demands in metropolitan areas of agro-industry. Being dominated by the colonial masters, these indigenous people have been pushed away from their lands because their lands have been taken away from them by the multinational companies seeking for the oil or timber. The Viracochas in The Storyteller signify the colonial masters who want to encroach upon the lands and territories of the native people for their trade. The reference to the "tree-bleeding" in the novel depicts the exploitation of the tribe by the Viracocha. These natives have their own stories in which they compare these viracochas with the Kamagarinis (servers of Demons). These viracochas when enter in their territories, trap the Machiguengas forcibly who have strong hands to bleed the trees. At the time when they start losing their strength, these viracochas get furious and in order to compensate for their own losses they start using "divide and rule" policy to make the natives bloodthirsty for each other. The natives consider land more than a physical entity because for them their land represents their identity and culture. In contemporary times, these indigenous people are being expelled from their territories by the wars and the corporations in order to extract natural resources. The distant regions of Amazon Forests are rich in beauty and resources and these regions are in danger due to their abundance in unknown treasures. The rich countries with the help of governments, armed forces, paramilitary and guerillas are doing massacre of the indigenous people in large number, stealing their land and culture in order to earn a profit by invading their lands. It is just like a holocaust for the uncontested indigenous people of the world. Saul in the novel supports his views about the indigenous by asking the narrator of the novel "Do our cars, guns, planes, and Coca-Colas give us the right to exterminate them because they don't have such things? Or do you believe in 'civilizing the savages,' pal? How? ... by forcing them to work on the farms as slaves to

Creoles like Fidel Pereira?... Making them zombies and caricatures of men..." (Llosa, 26). The natives have turned out to be internally displaced because they have been forced by the imperial powers to leave the lands for saving their lives.

The narrator in the novel tells that the indigenous people in the novel flee into the internal corners of the forests to save themselves, their culture, and traditions from the anthropologists but the efforts of these people are worthless. The narrator, after completing his project, starts hosting a TV show. During his hosting of a show, he comes in to contact with the Machiguengas. He notices an abrupt and huge change in their culture after the gap of twenty or thirty years. The dispersion that has characterized the life of the Machiguengas has come to an end. The little diasporic groups that have been scattered over here and there, having no contact with each other are terminated. These groups after the efforts of the authorities, missionaries, anthropologists and ethnologists have started developing the trade relations with the rest of Peru and they have been assimilated into the culture of each other. This depicts that these Machiguengas are slowly ceasing to be the primitive people. They have started making villages and communities. They have now established the caciques or the headman in their communities. But even after establishing these things, they have a feeling of isolation. This isolation is internal isolation as one cannot forget one's culture in just a few years. The narrator himself describes that "like other tribes, the Machiguengas were in the very midst of the process of acculturation: the Bible, bilingual schools, an evangelical leader, private property, the value of money, trade, Western clothes, no doubt..." (Llosa, 163).

The acculturation of the indigenous people reveals about the distorted relations between the centre and the periphery in this globalized world. This acculturation usually follows the direction in which minorities adopt the habits and culture of dominant groups but when there is no centre and periphery then the dominant groups also adopts the patterns of the minorities. However, in the case of the acculturation of the Machiguengas, it is a directed acculturation. This directed change occurs when the missionaries and the works of the other anthropologists and ethnologists establish dominance over the Machiguengas through military conquest or political control; thus making imperialism the most common precursor to directed change.

According to the model of dependency theory - centre and periphery, the indigenous people forms the outer part of the centre i.e. periphery and the rich countries from where these anthropologists and other missionaries come to culturally convert these people and in order to expose them to the trading globalized world, form the central part of the model. Dependency theory has a notion in which the "resources flow from a "periphery" of poor and underdeveloped states to a "core" of wealthy states, enriching the latter at the expense of the former. It is a central contention of dependency theory that poor states are impoverished and rich ones enriched by the way poor states are integrated into the "world system." This is what has been depicted in the novel. The Peruvian natives feel nowhere within their own lands because of the cultural conversion which can be related to the theory of centre and periphery. The narrator in the very last chapter of the novel himself admits that life in these regions has changed. It is not so like to increase the tourism here but to exploit these regions. The certain revolutionary detachments in this region like Sendero Luminoso movement, which have come down to the jungle have been bombarded by the Air Forces. The big nations and rich countries for their purposes want to exploit these countries and any kind of revolution is being quelled by them.

The Machiguenga are nomadic in their nature and have their own system of telling their myths, and traditions which have been now replaced by the globalized phenomena of popular culture. The imperial forces have exerted power on the natives by culturally converting them for their own purposes. The cultural hybridization has led these people on the verge of limbo in which they have neither totally accepted the new culture nor have left their traditional, old culture. Tasurinchi in the novel supports this view by apprising that "life gets difficult when a person goes to live somewhere else" (Llosa, 52). The narrator himself describes that despite centuries of explicit or implicit attempts to Occidentalize and Christianize the indigenous tribes, they remain a

"handful of tragic, indomitable beings, that society has broken up into tiny families, fleeing, always fleeing, from the whites, from the mestizos, from the mountain people, and from other tribes, awaiting and stoically accepting their inevitable extinction as individuals and as a group, yet never giving up their language, their gods, their customs." (Llosa, 162)

This metamorphosis of the culture of the natives can also be analyzed from the linguistic models of post-colonial writers especially of Bakhtin's idea of organic hybridity. The ongoing mixing of the language of the Natives and the Imperials has lead towards the changes in the verb system of the natives. It can be exemplified from the view of Mr Schneil's in the novel. He opines in the novel that the verb system of the Machiguengas was complicated and misleading because it mixed up the past and the present tenses. But after explaining the verb system of these Machiguengas, he gives examples to the narrator "of the humorous and unsettling implications of a form of speech in which before and now were barely differentiated" (93).

The novel suggests the impossibility of attaining one's authenticity in today's globalized world. Sommer in "Belonging and Bi-lingual States" has referred to the statement of Mario Vargas Llosa in which he has explained that "it is tragic to destroy what is still living, still a driving cultural possibility, but I am afraid we shall have to make a choice...where there is such economic and social gap, modernization is possible only with the sacrifice of the Indian cultures" (Sommer, 31). In the novel, the culture of the Machiguengas depicts that it has not been sacrificed by the natives but has become an inseparable part of the society as nationalities and identities have merged to make it practically impossible to grasp any kind of cultural authenticity, be it dominant or subaltern. The narrator feels nostalgic for the reality which now belongs to the past and cannot be regained.

Reinvigorating Identities in Ceremony

Born in 1948 In Albuquerque of New Mexico, Leslie Marmon Silko is a mixed ancestry Laguna-Pueblo, Mexican-White author. She lived with her family members for generations in Laguna Pueblo Reservation and she had learnt traditional stories and legends from her female family relatives. Her contribution to the revival of Native American Literature cannot be ignored as she has remained one of the key figures in the First Wave of the Native American Renaissance. The novel Ceremony was written in 1977 by her during the period of 1960's and 1970's. This period is referred to in the literature as a period of the Native American Renaissance. It refers to the literature of Native Americans which deals with the various facets connected to the culture, history, traditions and also to the life of Native Americans majorly in the past.

The term Native American Renaissance was first used by the critic Kenneth Lincoln in his book of the same name published in 1983. According to Kenneth Lincoln, the literature of Native American Renaissance is "a written renewal of oral traditions translated into Western literary forms" (Lincoln, 8). He has distinguished between the First and Second wave of Native American Renaissance by stating that the rebirth of Native American literature is "an attempt to recover traditions, beliefs, and even languages that were lost, suppressed, or marginalized during a centuries-long history of conquest that ended near close of the nineteenth century" (Henderson, 447). Suzanne Lundquist in Native American Literatures: An Introduction (2004) has suggested that there are three elements which define the period of Native American Renaissance, and these elements are - to reclaim the heritage through literary expressions, early texts to be re-evaluated by Native American Authors and to renew the interests in the artistic expressions of customary tribes.

The period of Native American Renaissance was the period of historical revisionism because the authors of this period tried to revive the history of invasion and colonization of the North American Continent. This historical revisionism inspired interest in Native cultures and in the communities of Native America. The writers of this period came up with longstanding roots of tribal myths and traditions. Leslie Marmon Silko also emerged as one of the important writers of Native America for her contribution in reviving the Native American Literature. She is widely acclaimed for her novels: Ceremony, Almanac of the Dead, Gardens in the Dunes and short story collections: Laguna Women: Poems, Western Stories, Storyteller (1981). She can certainly be regarded as the First Native American woman for making the oral literature accessible that has sustained Native Americans for a long period. Most of her works cover the theme of the survival of Native American identity in this world of globalization.

Broadly speaking, the term Native Americans has been used to define the indigenous people of Native America particularly, North America and South America. These natives are mostly for centuries have been linked to their lands. They have the internal and spiritual connection with their lands and nature. However, this connection was disturbed by the arrivals of the Europeans in the fifteenth century. During the late nineteenth century, many anthropologists began to write down the stories and languages that they had heard while examining the culture of Native Americans. For this reason, many of the stories are available for reading and appreciating the culture of Native Americans. Nevertheless, Native American Literature was not considered to be a valid literature because the literature was judged from the European notions and sensibilities. Traditional Native America has an oral history and Europeans did not consider it literature until it had been written in the form of a book and it was not until the 1960s and 1970s that Native American Literature recognized its literary value in the canon of World Literature.

The works of Leslie Marmon Silko reflects a profound understanding of Native American Literature. She has made a distinct and profound contribution to Native American culture and discourse. She has employed all the strategies with which she can preserve and maintain all the identities of her culture. Silko has such a knowledge inherent in the blood that she writes for her tradition, and her works are not only compatible with the worldviews of the Native Americans but also express ingeniously her messages, including Ceremony. Silko has made certain efforts to gain a wider readership which makes Ceremony one of the most significant novels written in the twentieth century.

Leslie Marmon Silko's Ceremony (1977) focuses on the theme of alienation in a culturally hybrid environment. Native Americans have been delineated as alienated due to the contacts of Europeans on their lands. The problem of alienation depicts that it has become impossible for the natives to maintain their traditions, and culture in modern life. Silko writes with a strong sense of affiliation with her native land and culture. As she belongs to the Laguna tribe of Pueblo people in west-central New-Mexico, she tries to preserve the traditions, myths and culture of this tribe in her novel Ceremony. The first confrontation between the Europeans and the Pueblos of New-Mexico took place some four centuries ago when the Spaniards came with the Coronado expedition in 1540. Later on, the power was used by the Spanish invaders in 1598 to make the Pueblos swear allegiance to the King of Spain. Silko's writing is full of all these ancestral experiences and as a result, her writing is enriched by indigenous and white influences.

Her novel focuses on the difference between mainstream American society and Native American society and tries to explore whether these societies in a hybrid society can be reconciled or not. It tries to reveal the clash of cultures in which there is a little understanding between these two cultures and their different facets, such as tradition, lifestyle and values. However, she has given instances in which it has been suggested in a lucid manner that the different cultures can and should interact.

The novel Ceremony represents Native Americans in a culturally hybrid environment and their ability to exist in a hybrid environment. Tayo, the protagonist of the novel, is a mixed-blood Native American struggling for his ancestry and his experiences of war-time and changing culture of Laguna. After returning to the poverty-stricken Laguna reservation, he continues to suffer from shell shock. The past memories of his cousin, Rocky as well his uncle who died in conflict during the World War II, haunt him day and night. For seeking relief from the mental illness of the World War II, he takes refuge in alcoholism. However, his old grandmother helps him to recover from his mental trauma with the help of medicine man, Betonie. Tayo, with the help of Betonie's rituals and ceremonies which have been changed according to the demand of time, becomes able to relieve himself from the mental trauma. Tayo comes to understand the world and his own place within the world as a Laguna man.

The novel tries to assert that the cultures which are intolerant of cultural diversity always lead towards destruction. This destruction can be shown through various instances in the novel. The profound insights of this matter can be analyzed from the characters having double-consciousness but are not able to comprehend anyone. Tayo's mental illness in the novel is not a result of shell-shock as it is understood at beginning of the novel. The roots of his mental illness can be traced back to his biological origin. It is revealed in the novel that Tayo is a hybrid of mixed-ancestry. His mother was a Native American and father was English. He stands on the border of two opposite cultures and is not able to grasp anyone. The mainstream American society regarded him as Native American while his own community disowned him. These two cultures are opposite to each other where one stands against the other. Tayo's hybrid identity becomes a matter of concern as it was one of the reasons for his mental trauma. The character Emo in the novel attacks him by saying as "there he is. He thinks he's something all right. Because he's part white. Don't you, half-breed?" (Silko, 57). Besides Emo, Tayo's aunt also discriminates with him for being a mixed-blood. She hates him because he is a half-breed and his mother brings disgrace upon the family by uniting with a white man. When his grandmother asks to perform a ceremony upon him for his recovery from trauma, she forcefully asserts that she does not think that ceremony can be performed on him because he is a half-breed. She frowns and gave an answer to the old grandma, "You know what people will say if we ask for a medicine man to help him. Someone will say it's not right. They'll say, 'Don't do it. He's not full blood anyway" (Silko, 33).

Tayo's situation has its direct relation with most of the Native Americans who also have double-conscious identities. Du Bois in *The Souls of Black folk* (1903) explained double consciousness as "sense of always looking at one's self through the eyes of others, of measuring one's soul by the tape of a world that looks on in amused contempt and pity" (Du Bois, location 85). This double consciousness has distorted Tayo's identity and he feels alienated in the mainstream American world and the Native American world.

Another typical case to represent the cultural variance in the novel can be examined from the concept of healing during Tayo's treatment in the hospital. While his treatment in the white men's hospital, he is divided into the two perceptions of "self" and "other." Janelle Palacios in "Traditional Storytelling in the Digital Era" has commented that the concept of healing has its associations with different perceptions of 'self'. For her, Americans tend to break self into parts: physical, emotional, spiritual; whereas, the self is integrated and perceived as a unit of the whole in American Indian view. She has also distinguished the Native American worldview from the Americans. She says while the Americans lay emphasis on the success of the individual, the Native Americans praise their oneness, balance, harmony and connectedness. Her arguments are reflected in the difficulties of Tayo to get recovered in the hospital. The reason for which Tayo doesn't get recovered is his sense of unity with the other members of tribes. The doctors teach him to think only about himself and about others in the hospital. They don't want him to use words like 'we' and 'us'. However, the ceremony helps him to understand that he is a part of "something larger and his cure would be found only in something great and inclusive of everything" (Silko, 126).

The destruction meted out in a culturally hybrid environment can be scrutinized in the novel through the character of Rocky and Tayo's mother, Laura. Both of them try to adopt the white men's culture of dominance and by refusing to accept the subordinate culture of their own. Tayo's mother, Laura remains spellbound by the white men and also entices the white men as she looks and dresses more like English women. She presumably wants to mimic the culture of her master and intentionally suppresses her cultural identity. Her desire to be a part of English society has brought disgrace to the whole community when she gives birth to Tayo out of marriage with a white man. For her behaviour, the native community believes that "what happened to the girl did not happen to her alone, it happened to all of them" (Silko, 69). Homi Bhabha in his essay "Of mimicry and man: The ambivalence of colonial discourse" posited that mimicry is often seen as something shameful and black or brown persons who engage in mimicry are always derided by other members of his or her group for doing so. Bhabha claimed this notion in words "the desire to emerge as 'authentic' through mimicry – through a process of writing and repetition – is the final irony of partial representation" (Bhabha, 126).

Like Laura, Tayo's cousin Rocky is also mesmerized by the culture of mainstream American society. He is averse to his native cultural values and traditions. His hostility towards celebrating the 'deer' pictures his hatred for the old custom of Pueblos. He makes fun of the native traditions because he believes in scientific explanations given to him in his school. His teachers at boarding school are proud of him and tell him that "nothing can stop you now except one thing: don't let the people at home hold you back" (Silko, 51). However, his charm for the white society leads towards his destruction. The war veterans in the novel have similar feelings for their native culture. They are excluded from public life and they spend most of their time in pubs by drinking and remembering their old days. In their old days, they experience respect and admiration for being a part of the mainstream American army but this respect and admiration of the white people for them is lost in the post-war period. The position of all these characters can be explained by giving reference of Homi Bhabha who has asserted that mimicry sometimes describes itself as unintentionally subversive. In his thinking, mimicry acts as a kind of performance which exposes the artificiality of all symbolic expressions of power and explains the hollowness of the codes of mimicked culture (Bhabha, 125).

The culturally hybrid environment in the novel can be perceived through the concept of individuality in Native American culture and mainstream American culture. In the novel Ceremony, the mainstream American society emphasizes the individuality of each person. The success of an individual is highly valued and it is all taught to the students in the boarding schools. The teachers mock at the traditions of the Native Americans and consider them superstitious. It can be seen in the science class where science teacher mocks at the "stupid old beliefs" of the Native Americans. The children get confused over two explanations, one which is given at home and another given at school. The children get influenced by school teaching and try to imbibe the values of American mainstream society. The example is of Rocky. He feels ashamed of his own culture at the school when the teachers teach the deplorable ways of the Native Americans. He rejects his ancestral traditions and tries to change his family views by forcing them to accept the scientific views which he learns from the school. The incident when Josiah reads the book about raising the cattle but then discarded the views of the books for raising the cattle, Rocky gets angry and tells that "those books are written by scientists. They know everything there is to know about beef cattle. That's the trouble with the way the people around here have always done things – they never knew what they were doing" (Silko, 76).

It can be examined that if the culture of the white men prefers individuality, the native culture lays stress on individualism. Tayo remains opposite to Rocky and his mother, Laura because he lays stress on individualism. He prefers that the tribal coherence is of higher significance than the individual one. Native Americans do not perceive a person as a single individuality. That's why Tayo's mother is not regarded as a single individuality by the village community. All people are ashamed of the ways of her lifestyle and they want her to accept the lifestyle and traditions of their own community. By her choice of men and lifestyle, the whole community feels ashamed because it is not a problem for her alone but is a problem of the whole community of tribe. For the members of the native community "what happened to the girl did not happen to her alone, it happened to all of them" (Silko, 69). Another instance of the tribal coherence is when Tayo completes the ceremony, he shares his story with other members and becomes acceptable in the society.

The difference in the cultures can be seen in the notion of their way of thinking for the health treatment of a patient. The Native American concept of health is different from American on the basis of spirituality. Tayo gives up his hope for living. His illness makes him feel tired. For the natives, a healthy person lives in harmony with the land. Tayo must cope with the past in order to feel whole. He needs to feel reunited with the land and other members of the community. The healing methods of natives are more efficient than others. Tayo in hospital get treated but he doesn't get better. He is sent to home anyway even when he cries "he cries all the time. Sometimes he vomits when he cries" (Silko, 16). The doctor at hospital forbids him to take Native American medicine. The Native Americans have the same feeling for the hospitals. These people don't trust their medicines and their method of treatment. The old man Betonie has a notion for hospitals. He says that it is a place where "they don't bury the dead, they keep them in rooms and talk to them" (123). The natives believe in the rituals of their culture to heal a person. The medicine which proves to be good for Tayo from recovering the traumas is the ancient ritual of the community. The natives treat a patient with politeness whereas the doctors in hospital treat them harshly. The example is when the medicine man Ku'oosh comes to meet Tayo for recovering him; he treats him with respect and politely asks about his illness. But when he comes to understand and recognizes that he cannot help him, he sends him to another medicine man, Betonie. He wants to make Tayo understand how ceremony works. He explains to him that ceremonies change and evolve; they are not the static ones "at one time, the ceremonies as they had been performed were enough for the way the world was then. But after the white people came, elements in this world began to shift; and it became necessary to create new ceremonies."

The success of ceremony and of Tayo's healing power depends on an understanding of what is of being important in his life and what should not be given importance in life. The important thing is that Tayo is associated with the challenging concepts of memory and he is not able to cope with his past. His memory doesn't function after the trauma of shell shock. He tries to forget the memories of the past but he remains unable in forgetting those memories. In order to get well, he has to cope with the past and he has to learn that he can trust his memory.

The hybrid environment which has caused a difference in the perceptions of Native American Identity and mainstream American society can further be examined on the basis of their relationship to the land. The relationship of natives to their land is crucial. They have an intimate relationship with the land but their relationship with the land gets disturbed during the colonial period. Many Native American characters in the novel cling to their past for their intimacy with their land. This land was stolen from them hundreds of years ago. They talk about land only in relation to the past. For war veterans, the land still belongs to them. The example that can here be referred is of Emo. He says while drinking "they took our land, they took everything" (55). But at the same time, he despises the land by calling it "old- dried- up thing" (25). This attitude of Emo reveals the clash with the old and traditional concepts of land in which natives see the land as a living being. The war veterans do not appreciate their land. The reason for this loss of interest in the land is because of the loss of interest in life after the trauma of the war. This loss is then preceded by their interest in the army and in the mainstream society of America. The war-veterans are rejected by the white society after the war because they are of no use to them. The character of Helen Jean in the novel also recognizes that the respect of the war veterans during the war is only because of their uniform. Now, they have been treated as nothing in society. It is their association with the respect that they want to possess the property on the American land. For them, the land is not what it is for their ancestors. The new generation only wants to gain a new identity of the dominant white society by rejecting the notions, values, traditions of their own native culture.

For the mainstream American society, the land is only an asset for the production of the things. They don't care about the beliefs and traditions of the natives regarding the land. The see land as a property and do not want to give something in return to the land. They do not have any gratitude for the land. The example can be revealed from the novel when the white people protect their land by using the fences during Tayo's search for the cattle. The manhandling of land is mostly revealed in the urban areas where the industries have been set up. These industries for their own purpose of trade not only exploit the lands but also disturb the ecological balance of the environment. Americans use the land to extract minerals for the production of armaments. The armament factory in the novel Ceremony uses Uranium as a source for the production of armaments. The manufacturing and testing of uranium have been witnessed by the family of Tayo and also by the other villagers. Tayo's grandmother describes it as "it was still dark; everyone else was sleeping. But as I walked back from the kitchen to my bed there was a flash of light through the window. So big, so bright even my old clouded up eyes could see it...I thought I was seeing the sun rise again, but it faded away..." (Silko, 245).

For natives, the land is something more than having only material value "there are some things more than money" (45). These natives find their intimacy with the land. Josiah says "this is where we come from, see. This sand, this stone, these trees, the vines, all the wildflowers. This earth keeps us going" (Silko, 45). Their relationship with the land is a comprehending part of their identity. The image of the spirit woman which Tayo sees in his dreams can be regarded as an example of how to treat a land properly. The people in Native America cope with the drought with their beliefs and customs. But when Tayo recalls the words of Emo it hurts him because he has a different attitude towards the land. He has heard Emo talking about the land of the Americans as "Indians have nothing compared to white people. He talks about their cities and all the machines and food they have, and take it from them" (Silko, 132).

The paradoxical nature of American society has created a culturally hybrid environment. Silko has opined that oral history and tradition form an integral part of the Native American society. This importance can be judged from the importance of ceremonies and rituals which are passed on from generation to generation by the mode of storytelling. It shows that Native American society is cyclic in its nature. The grandmother of Tayo reveals it by saying, "It seems like I already heard these stories before...only thing is, the names sound different" (Silko, 260). In its contrast, the white men's society of America is linear. It does not have a rich culture and wisdom like Native American culture. The history of America is tainted. It is because of its intervention in the global affairs of the world market. The legacies of America have been passed down but these are not fully passed down because they concentrate on the best and hide the shameful events. Native American history is not much valued in comparison to the American mainstream society. Native American history has much more wisdom than the history of America which is taught in the classes. The pitiable thing is that the history of American culture can be found in the classrooms across the countries but the history of Native Americans which is full of wisdom and has a rich cultural tradition is not preserved. Native Americans have to struggle hard to find their identity in this large complex world of globalization. It is only through their own efforts of indigenous survivance that they can preserve their lands, traditions and culture. It is paradoxical that Native Americans have to struggle for preserving their culture which is full of wisdom whereas American history which is edited is available for all to accept.

There are certain symbols in the novel which symbolizes the way in which whites of American society misunderstand the Native American society and making it hybrid in its own culture. They misjudged the traditions of Native America for their own purposes. It can be symbolized by the Gallup ceremony in the novel. This Gallup ceremony is organized every year by the white mayor and the council of Gallup. The wide range of Native American culture dancers are invited for Gallup ceremonial and they are paid for their performances. It demonstrates how the mainstream American society of whites is ignorant of the specific purpose of each ceremony. This ceremony is celebrated by the Americans purely for the purpose of entertainment by ignoring the purpose of the ritual which is celebrated by the natives around the important events of the year. The whites praise the artifacts of Native Americans only for their own purpose of entertainment by ignoring the ongoing lives of real Native Americans.

Silko in her novel tries to assert that though the culture of indigenous people, as well as of the white men, have a difference yet both communities have one element which connects these both societies. This element is of death. Death is present everywhere in the war. It is depicted when Tayo sees the dead soldiers; they all look dark after the death. It is supported by the feature when Tayo takes dead Japanese for his uncle Josiah. Hence, it can be concluded that the two communities in the novel can live in harmony if the culturally hybrid atmosphere created by them start considering the views of each other by living in harmony and mutual respect.

Scrutinization of Recurrent Patterns in

The Storyteller and Ceremony

The preceding chapters have been studied for the displaced identities in the culturally hybrid environment. The purpose of this chapter is to examine recurrent patterns in the two novels though the writers have been from different countries. The writers in the works have asserted their opinions regarding displaced native identities within their culturally hybrid territories. They have asserted that hybridism has become an inseparable part of their lives which has become a reason for the destruction and distortion of their culture and identities.

Mario Vargas Llosa in The Storyteller (1989) has described the exploration of the native's territories by the Christian missionaries, ethnographers and linguists who try their best to civilize and modernize the natives. Ceremony (1977) by Leslie Marmon Silko is also based on the same theme of natives who are searching for their identity in the mainstream American society. These novels mainly depict the process of globalization and how this process is continuously affecting the culture of the natives in the twentieth century with advancement in technology and expansion of the world trade. For the purpose of world trade and for gaining the power in hands, the imperial and colonial powers are exploiting the nature and lands of the indigenous and destructing their culture, making them displaced on their own lands. The Storyteller and Ceremony share the feature of displacement in the third world culture by having the stories which revolve around the characters who want to understand their role and place in this world. This chapter mainly focuses on the aspects which are common in both the novels. The commonality can be found on the basis of the elements of storytelling, the interference in the culture of the natives by Americans, the protagonists of both the novels have similarities as they have a quest to search their place and identity in their respective societies and the world.

The analysis and study of both novels reveal that the authors have shared a common ground by delineating the importance of storytelling in the culture of indigenous people. The element of storytelling in both the novels has exerted a dominant power on the protagonists. The element of storytelling, cultural exchange, and social activity form an essential part to deal with the imperial forces in order to construct the national and personal identity. Further, the storytelling has always remained a core and significant part to impart education and enjoyment to the indigenous people of the North and South America. The storytelling conveys the events in the words or in any other form whose only purpose is to educate and to give enjoyment to the listeners. The storytelling has predated the writing. Stories have been available in every culture whether it is modern or a primitive. The earliest form of storytelling was present in the oral form which can be combined with the gestures and expressions. As Salman Rushdie in his work Luka and the Fire of Life (2010) has explained that "man is the storytelling animal, and that in stories are his identity, his meaning, and his lifeblood" (Rushdie, 34).

The aboriginals of Australia paint the symbols of the story on the caves so that the story can be remembered by their group. The tattooing in some cultures also represents some form of stories. With the advent of the art of writing, the stories have been recorded in the books as a stable form and have been started reading by the people across the world. The tradition of oral storytelling is of much more important because it is developed by human beings after the initial paintings on the walls. When one speaks of the word "storytelling" it reminds us of the images from the image of a man sitting in front of the group and telling them stories. It is all known to us that history is written generally by those who are the victors of the world and they only present us the sanitized form of the stories. However, the art of oral storytelling provides the marginalized sections of the society a voice to keep alive their history and their actual self. It is in their collective consciousness that they have preserved the myths, rituals and legends.

With these entwining elements of myths, rituals, and legends, Llosa and Silko have consummated the subject of storytelling in their novels. Both novels deal with the progress of modernity and destruction of the cultures of the natives in the world. The destruction of their culture has been entwined in the form of stories by the novelists. Like many cultures in the world, the culture of the indigenous people of America has a preserved a strong element of the storytelling. They use storytelling as a way to pass down the customs, history, and heritage. Native Americans have a close intimation with their land, so storytelling becomes a necessary tool for them to pass down their traditions related to the customs of land that is how to live off from the land, and how to survive in the natural world. Nevertheless, with the interference of other nationalities which have started to settle down in their lands start exploiting these natives and forcibly relocate them into the territories of the land which are not their own. They preserve their identity by establishing a connection with each other through their customs, traditions and myths and rituals to keep alive their legacies through the storytelling. Through the medium of storytelling, the indigenous have kept their language alive and they have used the art of storytelling to preserve their traditions and history.

This tradition of storytelling has been depicted in both novels which have been taken for this project. In The Storyteller (1989), as the novel progresses, it starts informing readers about the myths and rituals of the Machiguengas. Their myths about the cosmos, the origin of the world, their gods and goddesses, their shamans both good and bad, the reason for their moving from one place to another are the core part of storytelling. Their myth of head- shrinking and how to control the anger are the part of their culture. Their relationship with the land and nature is brought out perfectly by the narrator. For them, getting angry is bad in their culture because if they get angry, it will disturb the balance of nature. The Machiguengas believe that anger can be a cause for the ruin and destruction of their culture and their lands. Their culture doesn't have a single storyteller. They have rather a set of people whose job is to keep moving and to update the people of that tribe about all the happenings in the other corners of the world. Tasurinchi, in the novel, is a name which symbolizes a person who tells stories to the members of the community about their moving. It is observed that the art of storytelling is not only kept safe by the indigenous people but it has been preserved by the urban storyteller, Saul Zuratas, as well who after getting influenced by their culture develops this art. However, his art of mixing and creating new stories makes him stand apart as the storyteller of the globalized world. In this way, he becomes an important figure among the natives as a source of entertainer and to inform them about the news of the world.

The urban man, Saul, turns into storyteller becomes an informer for the natives and suggest them cope with the circumstances in which these tribes are forced by the western societies to change themselves from the primitive stage of living to the modern ways of living. Although the changes happening in the globalized world are bringing changes in the primitive lifestyle of the natives yet the natives have preserved the art of storytelling in their collective consciousness. The instance of it is provided in the novel when the narrator asks the cacique of the tribe about the hablador. He doesn't reveal anything about him. The narrator explains that the Machiguengas utter the word 'hablador' with a great respect because for them he is the only person who can preserve the native culture which is embedded in their unconscious mind (Llosa, 91). The statement by the narrator reveals that though these natives have started trading and using money yet the weight of their traditions exerts a much stronger pull on them.

The importance of the hablador in the culture of Machiguengas can be analyzed from the point that the natives do not want to disclose any information to the missionaries about him. In the theories, which Mr Schneil's has developed about hablador, it is clearly indicated that hablador is like a courier service to the community of Machiguengas

the hablador, or habladores, must be something like the courier service of the community. Messengers who went from one settlement to another...keeping them informed of the happenings, the fortunes and misfortunes of the brothers...he is probably also the memory of the community, fulfilling a function similar to that of the jongleurs and troubadours of the Middle Ages. (Llosa, 93)

They think that if they will disclose any information about him then the missionaries will also destroy the hablador.

So, it's in their collective consciousness that they have tried to preserve the importance of hablador who tells them different tales for the preservation of their myths, their rituals, and their culture. For narrator, speaking the way like a storyteller speaks means " being able to feel and live in the very heart of that culture, means having penetrated its essence, reached the marrow of its history and mythology, given body to its taboos, images, ancestral desires, and terrors" (244).

Leslie Marmon Silko's Ceremony has also laid importance on the art of storytelling which is prevalent in every aspect of life. The novel has strong elements of the art of storytelling, and about the myths, rituals and ceremonies of Pueblo and Navajo people. Silko herself has said, "You don't have anything if you don't have the stories" (Silko, 2). The tradition of oral storytelling is inherent in almost all cultures. Silko has put the culture of oral storytelling in her novel for the subject matter. Throughout the novel, she has used storytelling for depicting the reciprocity of stories among the natives and Euro-Americans. After looking at the novel of Silko, one can definitely examine that story cannot be defined in a single dimension. The importance of storytelling in her novel can be illustrated from Thought Woman's perception for whom the stories have healing powers "they aren't just for entertainment. They are all we have, you see, all we have to fight off illness and death" (Silko, 2).

Silko has used the element of storytelling as a framework for her novel and it is scattered throughout the novel emphasizing the importance of storytelling in the Pueblo culture. she has tried to reveal to that the whites have attempted to destroy the ceremonies of the Pueblos but they have preserved their tradition of rituals, myths and witchery through an oral form of storytelling. To preserve their identity they have preserved the three important figures in the culture. The figures are of Thought Woman,

Corn Mother and Sun Father. The myths about these figures are important in two ways. At first, they explain the beliefs of Pueblos about the creation of the world and at second, they reveal the crucial element of storytelling in the Pueblo culture. The element of storytelling among Native Americans is more important for its mythical power than recreational value because it serves as a ceremony that serves a link between the mythical deities and the natives. There exists a relationship between the deities and the natives because the ceremonies are performed by the people to meet their needs. The element of storytelling plays an important part through the use of ceremonies in the novel. In the novel, Pueblos and Navajos posit that these stories are the ways for Native Americans to explain everything that they know about the universe.

Silko has suggested that storytelling acts in a circular and non-linear way. The words of the Thought Woman illustrate the circularity and non-linearity of the stories with the interweaving of time and memory. The stories have the power to pass the myths of the creation from generation to generation. These stories act as a thought of imagination. Its circular motion has been examined through the structure of the novel where the stories of Thought Woman are intertwined with the life of Tayo. The circular motion of storytelling becomes an aid for Tayo to heal himself from his mental illness. Silko's view in Philomena Mariani's Critical Reflections: The Politics of Imaginative Writing (1998) reveals the significance of storytelling where she has asserted that "the stories are always bringing us together, keeping this whole together, keeping this family together, keeping this clan together. 'don't go away don't isolate yourself because we've all had these kinds of experiences" (Silko, 86).

It has been analyzed that besides the element of storytelling, the novels have focused upon similar themes as well. Over the years, the countries of Latin America and North America have developed several themes which are very complex and are related to the policy of 'mestiza.' Basically, the themes are related with the natives of the lands who are facing an abrupt kind of destruction to their culture from the imperial powers of Euro-American countries. These forces for their own purposes are destructing the lands and culture of these natives. These powers for making themselves more powerful are indirectly dominating the natives of the lands at the name of Christianizing and making them modern. However, the strategies employed by them have resulted in the suppression of the natives. The indigenous people have developed hybrid identities seeking for their place in the world which has been converted through the powers of mainstream American society. The natives have been acculturated by the whites and they are living in a total isolation. The reason for this isolation is because of their rejection to accept the culture of mainstream American society and refusal to leave their own primitive culture and traditions.

Latin American natives for most of the times have been conquered by the Spanish missionaries, resulting in the acculturation of these natives. Mario Vargas Llosa in his novel The Storyteller (1989) has dealt with the theme of acculturation and displacement of the indigenous tribe of the Amazon Forests of Peru. The novel depicts that these tribes have been "literally decimated" and are on the point of disappearing (Llosa, 80). The novel deals with the Machiguenga tribe of Amazon Forests in Peru who are nature-oriented, non-violent and are nomadic. These natives during the boom period in Latin America have been displaced at frequent intervals by the "warlike tribes and by whites" (82). The narrator argues that socialism will make possible the co-existence between modern and primitive Peru. The industrial development in the parts of Peru has inevitably annihilated the culture of the Machiguengas. The primitive Machiguengas are the worst victims of exploitation and cruelty by the Dominican missionaries, linguists and ethnographers who tortured these people for their own motive. The characters like Jum in the novel are the example of bearing this torture. He has been tortured by the party of whites and mestizos who come in Urakusa for a trade. They beat Jum and torture him in the public. The whites burn all the huts of the Indians, beat them mercilessly and rape several women. For the whites, Jum is capable to teach the people of his tribe about the instructions of the linguists. However, Jum is aware of the consequences of this program. The Amazonian tribes do not attain the goal of the program but this program has attained the far-reaching consequences. The natives of the Amazon forests find that they have been exploited by the traders with whom they trade. The narrator illustrates the purpose of The Summer Institute of Linguistics which is a part of the policy of American Imperialism. This institution under the name of doing "scientific research," has taken a step towards neocolonialist "penetration of the cultures of the Amazonian Indians" (71). This institute, as a part of American Imperialism, has attempted to westernize the aboriginal cultures and exploit them for a mercantile economy. The power of imperialists is just converting the culture of these people in to "zombies." The cultural conversion leads to the displacement of the Machiguengas who are searching for their place in the globalized world where imperial forces in Peru are exploiting the lands of these people by imposing their culture on them.

This theme of the destructiveness of the culture of Native America by mainstream American society has found a place in Leslie Marmon Silko's Ceremony. Ceremony has the theme of the preservation of the traditions and culture of Native American Pueblos against the Imperial American society. The Pueblos came in to contact with the whites in the sixteenth century. The control over Pueblo region by the settler states had influenced the tradition, languages, and natural resources of the region. This novel demonstrates Silko's concern with Native American culture by making people aware of the reality of the cultural mixing. Tayo, the main character in the novel, reveals the cultural mixing of the two societies – one, the Native American and the second, the mainstream American society. Silko has revealed this aspect as a painful moment of life because living as a mixed blood in Laguna society means not to be fully accepted either by the full-blooded Native Americans or the white people. The lack of acceptance by both societies becomes a reason for the distortion of Tayo's identity.

In the novel, the war-veterans get respect in the mainstream American society only when they wore American uniforms during World War II. Nevertheless, their position was changed when the war gets over. They do not receive the same kind of respect which they received when they were fighting from the side of America. "...It was white people who gave them that feeling and it was white people who took it away again when the war was over" (Silko, 43). So, this statement reveals the attitude of the white Americans who have used the natives for their own purpose and when their mission turns successful they discard them. The towns of America attract the younger generation for white-collar jobs with good pay, but the problem of racism denies for giving them any such position. The natives who become able to gain jobs for earning start spending money in the bars on alcoholism. This process reveals that the racist policies of the imperial powers want to dominate the structure of the world by becoming more powerful and by imposing their powerful values of white culture on them; they have brought destruction to the identities of the colonized.

The works for the cause of indigenous people have always tried to present the protagonists or other characters in search for their identity. This search for identity remains the main motif for the writers to present the protagonist in the modern complex world of globalization. This motif for the quest of identity by the protagonists has found its place in the novels of Mario Vargas Llosa and Leslie Marmon Silko. The protagonist of Mario Vargas Llosa's novel The Storyteller is analyzed from this point of view. The position of the protagonist in the novel The Storyteller is made viable by the narrator himself and by Saul Zuratas. Both of them are the students of ethnography that study the people and their cultures. Being the students of ethnography, they focus their research on the Amazonian tribe of Machiguengas. The narrator's interest in doing the research on these tribes is scientific. He has no personal intimation with them. On the other hand, the interest of Saul in these tribes is more than scientific because he has certain intimation with them for being considered as 'other'. His interest can be considered as a spiritual as he develops a deep connection with them because of their exploitation and their displaced identity in their own culture and territory. He feels this displacement in his own identity also. He has a huge birthmark on his face which gives him a bizarre appearance. His birthmark has earned him a name 'Mascarita'. His association with Jewish religion becomes a great problem for him. Saul's ugly appearance and relationship with Jewish religion have made him displaced in his own society. Even his father does not want him to sit in his shop because his appearance will frighten the customers and they will not come to his shop. His own displacement in the society makes him interested in the Amazonian tribe of Machiguengas. Although he is timid yet he is deeply concerned about the indigenous and he strongly criticizes those missionaries who on the name of making them civilized are actually exploiting them. In college days, he becomes an object of ridicule because of his resentment against the missionaries. His resentment against the missionaries makes him abandon the ethnology which lacks interest in the morality of pure cultures. Eventually, he becomes interested in the Machiguengas and their beliefs. He travels to the forest many times and starts getting interested in their culture.

Another thing for which he gets interested in their culture is due to his acceptance by the Machiguengas which he does not find in his own society because of his ugly appearance. He is physically and socially outcasted from his society and in the same way the Machiguengas are also outcasted by the missionaries who want to exploit their lands at the name of civilization. Though these Machiguengas kill their children who are born disfigured yet they accept Mascarita because he influences them with the stories of the Metamorphosis and the exodus of Jews. He realizes his intimation with these tribal people for they have also been alienated by the white men's society. He does not show his resentment against the society which comments on him rather he shows his resentment indirectly by mixing and adopting the culture of the Machiguengas. He becomes the storyteller for the Machiguengans, the man who wants to preserve the age-old traditions of the Machiguengas, no doubt by mixing them with the western stories. He finds his place and identity with those Machiguengas because they have accepted him even because of his flaws which the mainstream society does not accept. He is the character who finally finds his place by becoming one with the Machiguengas. His quest for identity is completed at last when he leaves his modern society, his friends and also his research as an ethnographer to get himself absorbed in the culture of the Machiguengas. His journey is the story of a man who weaves the mysteries of identity through storytelling and creates a spellbinding tale from the modern world into the origins of the man.

This quest for identity has also found its place in Leslie Marmon Silko's Ceremony (1977). Tayo, the protagonist, is half-white and half-native which become a reason for his identity crisis. He has a feeling of displacement because he feels that he doesn't belong to either of the cultures. He undergoes a figurative journey in which he transforms his identity fully as a Native American. He becomes able to develop his identity in the two conflicting cultures. His journey involves several steps which help him to revive his native identity of native America. It is observed that when violence destroys the identity of a person as well as the understanding of a person about what it means to be a human, from that point onwards, a person starts his journey to rediscover and remake his identity. This is what that happens in the novel Ceremony when the realization of Tayo is broken when the Japanese enemies look like his uncle Josiah. He remains unable to kill them in the novel and it is with the death of Rocky that he loses his sense of self-worth. His sickness is not a classic tale of alienation. His journey in the novel to find his place in society can be regarded as a ritual quest because he has to reunite with his Laguna. His journey also becomes a spiritual journey because he has to achieve salvation that can only be completed by overcoming his past traumas and by accepting his mixed cultural heritage. His first step towards his salvation or the search for identity starts when he returns from the war and is haunted by the memories of the past that are full of devastation. He is suffered from the haunts of evil and his inability to control himself.

However, he becomes successful when the guardian of his soul, medicine man, guides him throughout his journey for the freedom of his spirit. The medicine man performs a ceremony on him which leads to the crossing of the threshold of the beliefs. He develops a different positive attitude in his life. With this possession of positive attitude of wisdom, he regains his strength of making his final step to the journey of self-recovery. He returns to Ku'oosh for attaining new wisdom who asks him to drink the water cupping it in the hands (Silko,258). After this possession of positive attitude, he shares a balance between the two worlds i.e. real and spiritual world. He starts sharing love and happiness with the people who surround him and he starts controlling his will and spirit. It is by following these steps that become able to discover his self in the native tradition of Laguna-Pueblo origin.

These similarities among both the novels have revealed that the fate of the indigenous due to the contacts established by the settler states, colonizers, missionaries and the linguists. With the contact of the various missionaries and colonizers, the new generation of the indigenous is suffered from distorted identities where they are keen to find their originality searching which has become unacceptable in the white society.

Conclusion

The distortion of identities due to cultural displacement, which can be illustrated as the physical dislocation from one's own native culture and the land by imposement of the foreign imperial policies of colonization, is the most burning issue of the today's era. The writers from the indigenous communities are trying to depict and have made possible attempts to reveal that when a person leaves one's culture and experiences the culture of the other communities always finds himself trapped nowhere. The uprooting from one's own culture at the name of the modernization and civilization is the hardship that is being faced by the indigenous people from various countries. A general question arises here is that whether the colonial or imperial forces at the name of the democratic character of the development are actually developing them or not? The only answer to this is no. The institutes and the imperial forces at the name of making the barbarians civilized are actually exploiting them and making them their culture and identities supersede with their cultural values. The imperial forces design many plans to develop the economy of indigenous people by introducing the concept of new market and by using their lands. However, it has been observed that the imperial and colonial forces have just exploited the resources and the natives for their own benefits. These forces use to work by implying the ideology of civilization to dominate the people at the name of education, and modernity. This ideology of indirectly dominating the indigenous of Latin America has been used as a theme in the works of different indigenous writers of the world.

During the analysis of the works, it has been scrutinized that the countries of North and South America have shared a same political past of colonialism, dictatorships, of communism and of a complex power dynamic with both United States and European powers. The power of colonialism has always oppressed the indigenous by maintaining the class difference and racial discrimination. It is not only limited to the oppression but also to sexual exploitation and repression of the women of indigenous and all these suppressions have emerged to subjugate the indigenous peoples. This suppression has been ranging from labour exploitation to the tax payments and further, to the confiscation of the lands and other natural resources to the genocides of the indigenous peoples. In the present scenario, there are many factors which can be considered for the displacement of the identities of the indigenous of Latin America and for their suppression. The first one among them is the increasing urbanization. The indigenous peoples feel a strong attachment to their rural territories, but for their livelihood, they have to live in the urban territory which has resulted in losing their connection with their own lands and culture. It is the problem which makes them displaced from their own culture. New considerations have been added into their lives which have made their fate more individualized. Another factor which can be considered for the displacement of the indigenous is the extraction of the resources from the lands of these peoples which is posing a threat to their rights for the land. The governments of the Amazonian regions and of other regions of Latin America are inviting the new companies from the mainstream American society for new investments. It is with the new intergovernmental trade agreements in which the forces from the developed countries have facilitated the work of extraction of the resources from the lands of the indigenous people without any consultation with these people. The result is the dispossession and exclusion from their lands. The indigenous people living in isolation in the inner inaccessible regions of the Amazon rainforests have been pushed away by the activities of oil and gas companies. These people don't want to come into contact with the national society but when they get excluded from their territories, they start moving to the other regions where they have to adopt a new culture of that region. It just makes them hybrid in their identities, where they can neither adjust themselves to the new climate and culture nor can they leave behind their own culture. The persistent racism and ethnicity have led to the new level of inequality and conflict among these indigenous people.

By keeping in mind these problems of the indigenous culture, the theory given by Homi K. Bhabha in his The Location of Culture has been examined to explain the cultural identity of the indigenous. These terms have been so far used in this research for explaining the relevance of the concepts in relation to the indigenous peoples of America. To contemplate upon the political and cultural displacement problems, the author Mario Vargas Llosa and Leslie Marmon Silko have taken these issues in their particular novels. The first chapter of the thesis has dealt with Vargas Llosa's novel The Storyteller which is inspired by the author's own perception of the Peruvian society. Basically, in his works, he has criticized the works of the governments and the institutes which at the name of making these indigenous people civilized and modern are actually exploiting them. The novel has depicted the political turmoil in Latin America. As it is discussed earlier that Llosa himself is a Peruvian, so he knows very well the problems of the natives and indigenous living there.

The Storyteller shows that the works of the imperial forces have made the indigenous of the Amazon forests displaced identities. His character Saul Zuratas from the city life and the tribe of Machiguengans in the Amazonian rainforests are the examples of the displaced identities. In the case of Saul, his outlook has made him socially outcast. His bizarre appearance has made him a sympathetic character. He searches for his identity in society because of two reasons. The first one is that his mother belonged to the Christian background and his father to the Jewish. The second is because of his huge birthmark on his face. He, for the search of his identity in a cultural hybrid environment, has explored his situation likewise with those Amazonians. Then, the situation of these Amazonians has also been explored in the cultural hybrid environment where there is an impossibility to maintain a pure identity in this globalized world. The situation of these Amazonians is pitiable because they have been exploited by the Christian missionaries and the linguists. The encounter of the Amazonians with the colonizers and missionaries has made them experience traumatic events in their lives. With the encounters of these missionaries, they become prone to the diseases of the new kinds because their immune system is not developed to fight with the diseases like cold, measles or diarrhoea. The works of the anthropologists to study these tribes have just made them flee from their lands to save their culture. So, one can estimate from these things the terrible condition of the Amazonians who are fleeing to the inner corners of the forests to save themselves from getting culturally hybrid.

In a similar way, the culturally hybrid identities have also shown in the novel of Leslie Marmon Silko's Ceremony. The novel mainly has illustrated the concept of the "clash of the cultures." It has depicted what happens when the two different cultures from different regions, one dominating and another subordinate one, clash with each other. This impact can be analyzed from the different mental stresses, disappointments in the life, alcoholism, and from the losing interest in life. The person from a society, who is of mixed origin, faces a lot of problems. The author herself is a culturally hybrid has to face displacement in the society because of non – acceptance from the members of the society. Native Americans face a conflict in their consciousness. This double consciousness can be reflected through their psyche and their habits. Silko has used this problem of double consciousness in her novel because she herself was of a mixed breed. She has explained this hybridity through her character Tayo, who is of mixed origin. His character signifies those natives who have to face two different cultures in society. There are some natives in the society who choose the culture of mainstream American society because they feel ashamed of their own culture. The characters of Rocky and Tayo's mother, Laura are the best examples. There are also those natives who because of the frustrations of the mainstream American society want to go back and also want to adopt the traditions of their own culture. The character of Tayo in Leslie Silko's novel is the best example.

The novels have been compared on the basis of the various common elements present in both of the novels. These elements have been compared on the basis of similarities. The similarities have been analyzed and compared on the basis of storytelling element which is prevalent in the culture of the indigenous and both writers have used this element in their novels. The themes of the novels also share a similarity in reference to the displaced identities of the indigenous. The protagonists of both novels also bear a similarity. These both protagonists search for their identity in this multicultural world of globalization.

The writers in their novels show that these indigenous people feel some kind of alienation with their own culture due to unnecessary interference by the imperial and colonial powers. These colonial powers tend to exclude their statements about the exploitation of the colonized and their resources at the name of the private politics for the development of these indigenous. These colonial powers tend to focus on the barbaric depravity of colonized people and they use to conceal the benefits which they derive by exploiting the lands of the indigenous. It is with this problem to maintain an original identity of that certain resistance movements in the twenty-first century have arisen in the different regions of Latin America by these natives and indigenous to protect themselves and their culture, traditions, values and their lands from the forces of imperials. Latin America has witnessed a lot of leftist movement with which indigenous are responding to the overall changes in social, political and economic policies. These indigenous movements are related to the political scene in Latin America itself and on the other hand, these movements have also the relationship with the other movements on the globe. These movements of the indigenous according to social movement theory are due to the relative deprivation or inequalities faced by these indigenous. These movements with a special effect are challenging to the neoliberal policies of the government which allows for exploiting the land of the indigenous. The certain Amazonian movements claim for their own autonomy in the economy and in other fields also. The conflict in 2009 of El Baguazo that was the military intervention was due to the opposition between the governments and indigenous for their opposition against the ongoing activity of oil extractives. The other movements like the Zapatista movement or the Guerilla Warfare are some of the resistance movements which are adopted by the indigenous to save their lands and their culture from the forces of the United States which are exploiting them for their own benefits. These certain movements have recognized their importance in the culturally hybrid identities of the Latin American indigenous peoples. These strategies have been adopted by the indigenous for their own rights to claim that their

lands, their culture and traditions which are vital for their existence. The rights of the indigenous have granted them the right to self-determination so that they can maintain their original identities and their culture.

Pictorial Representation of Indigenous Americans

NATIVE AMERICANS AT THE WHITE HOUSE FOR CITIZENSHIP: A GLANCE

Image: 1. Native Americans Posing for Photograph During 1915

Image: 2. Native American Woman Meeting US President Calvin Coolidge for Indian Citizenship Act in 1923

Image: 3. Image of Indigenous Women, Travelled to Washington DC to Celebrate Newly Signed Indian Citizenship Act in 1924

Image: 4. Native American Men, Women and Children in Washington DC to Speak to President Coolidge in 1924

Image: 5. . Native American elder photographed during 1925

Image: 6. Native Americans at White House in 1929

Image: 7. Two Native American Elders in Discussion with Member of President Coolidge's Staff

Image: 8. A group of Native Americans Raising the United States Flag at the Lincoln Memorial in 1936

Image: 9. Three young Native Americans pictured using bicycle for the first time in 1938

Image: 10. President Coolidge with Native American Tribes

Image: 11. Native Americans Pictured with President Calvin Coolidge on the White House lawn

Image: 12. Image Portraying an Igloo and Eskimo Family

UNCONTACTED INDIGENOUS TRIBES OF AMAZON FOREST: A GLANCE

Image: 1. Members of Indigenous Tribe Staring at Aircraft in the Amazon Region

Image: 2. Members of Indigenous Tribe with Basket Full of Manioc and Papaya Fresh from Their Garden

Image: 3. Tribal Members Appear Defensive From the Air

Image: 4. Uncontacted Jururei Indigenous Woman in Rondonia Territory

References

Andersson, Vibeke. "Indigenous People – Territory and Identity: The Case of Bolivia". Transforming Landscapes of Poverty, Norway, 2005. Print.

Bakhtin, Mikhail. "Discourse in the Novel". The Dialogic Imagination: Four Essays. Trans. Caryl Emerson and Michael Holquist. USA: University of Texas Press, 1981. Print.

Bhabha, Homi. The Location of Culture. New York: Routledge, 1994. Print.

Brazilian Indian Protection Foundation. "A 2008 photo showing members of a recently discovered indigenous tribe, with their bodies painted in bright red staring at the aircraft from which the pictures were taken, in the Amazon region in the Brazilian-Peruvian border." news.com, AFP, 2008, <https://www.news.com.au/technology/environment/natural-wonders/inside-the-mysterious-world-of-the-amazons-last-uncontacted-tribes-where-thousands-still-live-in-total-isolation-unaware-of-modern-life/news story/8dfac22c939cd982003c86b36554b9b2.html.>.

Brown, Dee. Bury My Heart at Wounded Knee: An Indian History of the American West. New York: Henry Holt and Company, 2007. Print.

Cancilini, Nestor Garcia. Hybrid Cultures: Strategies for Entering and Leaving Modernity. US: University of Minnesota Press, 1995. Print.

Cohen, Robin. "Creolization and Cultural Globalization: The Soft Sounds of Fugitive Power". Globalizations. Vol.4, no. 3, 2007, 369-384. Pdf.

Chavkin, Allan. Leslie Marmon Silko's Ceremony: A Casebook. New York: Oxford University Press, 2002. Print.

Du Bois, W. E. B. The Souls of Black Folk. New York: Dover Publications, 1903. Kindle file.

Echevarria, Roberto Gonzalez, Enrique Pupo-Walker. The Cambridge History of Latin American Literature. UK: Cambridge University Press, 1996. Print.

Flavin, Francis. "Native Americans and Native History." tDAR: The Digital Archaelogical Record. Arizona State University: 2004. Pdf file.

Guignery, Vanessa, et.al. Hybridity: Forms and Figures in Literature and the Visual Arts. UK: Cambridge Scholars Publishing, 2011. Print.

Helmer, Matthew. "The Indian Civil Rights Act of 1968." study.com. N.d: N.pag. Web. 23 December, 2017. < https://study.com/academy/lesson/the-indian-civil-rights-act-of-1968.html>.

Leonard, Royston. "A group of Native American men wearing their traditional attire while raising the Stars and Stripes at the Lincoln Memorial in 1936, 12 years after President Calvin Coolidge granted them US citizenship." vintage everyday, Daily Mail, Media Drum World, May 25, 2018, <https://www.vintag.es/2018/05/native-americans-at-white-house.html>.

---. "Native Americans at the White House, circa 1929." vintage everyday, Daily Mail, Media Drum World, May 25, 2018, <https://www.vintag.es/2018/05/native-americans-at-white-house.html>.

---. "Native Americans posing for group portrait in 1915." vintage everyday, Daily Mail, Media Drum World, May 25, 2018, <https://www.vintag.es/2018/05/native-americans-at-white-house.html>.

---. "Pictured is President Calvin Coolidge with a group of Native Americans on the White House lawn." vintage everyday, Daily Mail, Media Drum World, May 25, 2018, <https://www.vintag.es/2018/05/native-americans-at-white-house.html>.

---. "President Coolidge with Native American tribes, 1924." vintage everyday, Daily Mail, Media Drum World, May 25, 2018, <https://www.vintag.es/2018/05/native-americans-at-white-house.html>.

---. "This remarkable photograph shows Native American men, women, and children in Washington D.C., to speak to President Coolidge. In 1924, Coolidge signed the Indian Citizenship Act, granting citizenship to indigenous people. Well-deserved: they had been in the country for generations before the "Americans" who automatically receive citizenship at birth." vintage everyday, Daily Mail, Media Drum World, May 25, 2018, <https://www.vintag.es/2018/05/native-americans-at-white-house.html>.

---. "This Native American elder was photographed around 1925." vintage everyday, Daily Mail, Media Drum World, May 25, 2018, <https://www.vintag.es/2018/05/native-americans-at-white-house.html>.

---. "Two Native American elders, dressed in traditional garb discussing policy with a member of President Coolidge's staff." vintage everyday, Daily Mail, Media Drum World, May 25, 2018, <https://www.vintag.es/2018/05/native-americans-at-white-house.html>.

---. "These Native American women traveled to Washington DC in 1924 to celebrate the newly-signed Indian Citizenship Act." vintage everyday, Daily Mail, Media Drum World, May 25, 2018, <https://www.vintag.es/2018/05/native-americans-at-white-house.html>.

---. "This Native American woman, center is meeting US President Calvin Coolidge in 1923 in advance of the Indian Citizenship Act." vintage everyday, Daily Mail, Media Drum World, May 25, 2018, <https://www.vintag.es/2018/05/native-americans-at-white-house.html>.

Llosa, Mario Vargas. The Real Life of Alejandro Mayta. USA: Farrar, Strauss and Giroux, 1984. Print.

---. The Storyteller. USA: Farrar, Straus and Giroux, 1989. Print.

Miranda, Gleison. "The photos reveal a thriving, healthy community with baskets full of manioc and papaya fresh from their gardens." survivalinternational, FUNAI, May, 2018, <https://www.survivalinternational.org/tribes/uncontacted-brazil.html.>.

---. "Uncontacted Indians in Brazil appear defensive from the air. This photo was taken in 2008." Survivalinternational, FUNAI, May, 2018,

<https://www.survivalinternational.org/tribes/uncontacted-brazil.html.>.

Mariani, Phil. Critical Fictions: The Politics of Imaginative Writing. New York: Bay Press, 1991. Print.

Mosteller, Kelli. For Native Americans, Land Is More Than Just The Ground Beneath Their Feet. Not Even Past, October 26, 2016. Web. September 9, 2018.

Ocasio, Rafael. Literature of Latin America. London: Greenwood Press, 2004. Print.

Palacios, Janelle. "Traditional Storytelling in the Digital Era." Fourth World Journal 11.2 (2012): 41-56. Print.

Public Domain. "This image claims to portray an igloo and Eskimo family standing outside it, taken at an unknown date." dailymail, mediadrumworld. September 13, 2017,

<https://www.dailymail.co.uk/news/article-4879836/Historic-photos-Indigenous-People-world.html.>.

---. "Two Worlds Collide: Three young native Americans reportedly pictured using a bicycle for the first time in 1938." dailymail, mediadrumworld. September 13, 2017, <https://www.dailymail.co.uk/news/article-4879836/Historic-photos-Indigenous-People-world.html.>.

Remp, Katelyn. "Using the Land to Heal: A Warrior's Journey in Leslie Marmon Silko's Novel Ceremony." Ecospirit 6.4 (N.d.): n,pag. Pdf file.

Romberg, Raquel. "Revisiting Creolization". Sounding Board. 2002: N.pag. Web. May 24, 2018. <https://www.sas.upenn.edu/folklore/center/ConferenceArchive/voiceover/creolization.html.>.

Rushdie, Salman. Luka and Fire of Life. London: Jonathan Cape, 2010. Print.

Silko, Leslie Marmon. Ceremony. New York: Penguin, 1986. Print.

Sommer, Doris. "Be-longing and Bi-lingual States." Diacritics. Vol.29, no.4, 1999, 84-115. Print.

St. Andrews. "Healing the Witchery: Medicine in Silko's Ceremony." Arizona Quarterly. 14 (1988): 86-94. Web. September 5, 2018.

Strizova, Tereza. The Clash of Two Cultures in Ceremony. Diss. Masaryk University, 2013. Pdf.

Teal, Whitney. "Hispanista: the Latin American Boom". Uptown Literati. April, 2010: N.pag. Web. May 23, 2017. <https://uptownliterati.wordpress.com/2010/04/02/hispanista-the-latin-american-boom/.html>.

The Nobel Prize in Literature 2010. NobelPrize.org. Nobel Media AB 2017. Oct 27, 2017. <https://www.nobelprize.org/prizes/literature/2010/summary/.html>.

Vargas, Rogerio. "Uncontacted Jururei Indian woman in the Urueu Wau Wau indigenous territory, Rondônia, Brazil." survivalinternational, FUNAI, May, 2018, <https://www.survivalinternational.org/tribes/uncontacted-brazil.html.>.

Yale School of Forestry & Environmental Studies. "History of Settlement in the Amazon Basin". The Global Atlas. 2018: N.pag. Web. May 23, 2018.

<https://globalforestatlas.yale.edu/amazon/land-use/history-amazon-settlement.html>.

Young, Robert J.C. Colonial Desire: Hybridity in Theory, Culture and Race. London: Routledge, 1995. Print.